TEMPERATURE

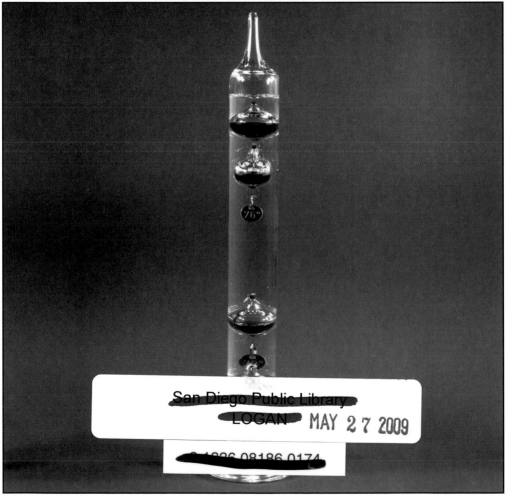

Navin Sullivan

 **Marshall Cavendish**
Benchmark
New York

Marshall Cavendish Benchmark
99 White Plains Road
Tarrytown, New York 10591-9001
www.marshallcavendish.us

Library of Congress Cataloging-in-Publication Data
Sullivan, Navin.
Temperature / by Navin Sullivan.
p. cm. — (Measure up!)
Summary: "Discusses heat, temperature, the science behind measuring
temperature, and the different devices used to measure
temperature"--Provided by publisher.
Includes bibliographical references and index.
ISBN-13: 978-0-7614-2322-5
ISBN-10: 0-7614-2322-2
1.   Heat--Juvenile literature. 2. Thermometers--Juvenile literature. 3. Temperature--Juvenile literature. I. Title. II. Series:
Sullivan, Navin. Measure up!
QC256.S85 2007
536'.5--dc22
2006011981

Editor: Karen Ang
Editorial Director: Michelle Bisson
Art Director: Anahid Hamparian
Series Designer: Alex Ferrari
Photo research by Iain Morrison

Cover: PictureQuest / Steve Allen

The photographs in this book are used by permission and through the courtesy of:
Peter Arnold, Inc.: Leonard Lessin, *1. Corbis:* Paul Seheult/Eye Ubiquitous, 8; Craig Aurness, 9; David Lees, 12; Bettmann, 14, 28; Roger Ressmeyer, 15. *Index Stock Imagery, Inc.:* Katie Deits, 37. *Photo Researchers, Inc.:* Ted Kinsman, 4; Mauro Fermariello, 6; Gusto, 11; Alan Sirulnikoff, 23; Stephen & Donna O'Meara, 27; Maximilian Stock Ltd., 29; NASA, 33; Jeff Lepore, 35; Peter Bowater, 42; Andrew Lambert Photography, 44. *Phototake:* Carol and Mike Werner, 43. *PictureQuest:* Hal Lott/Stock Connection, 10; Eric Futran/FoodPix, 24; BananaStock, 38. *Science Photo Library:* Adrienne Hart-Davis, 26; Andrew Lambert Photography, 31, 32.

Printed in China
3 5 6 4 2

Contents

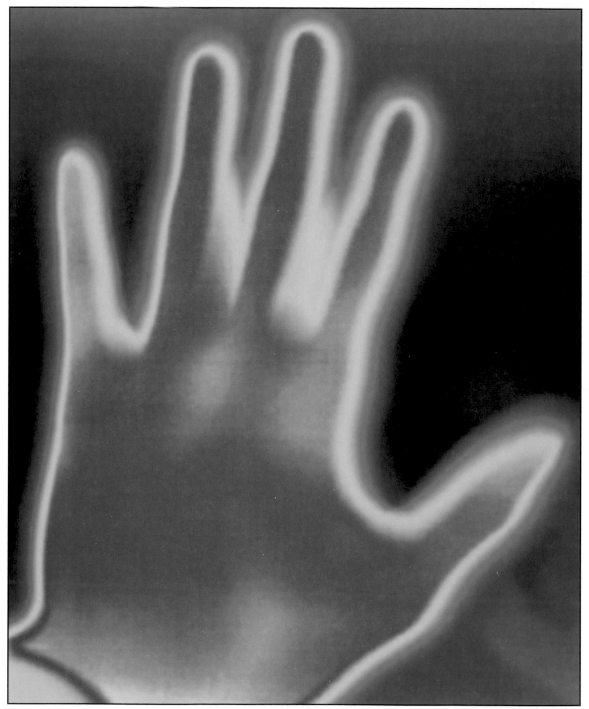

A special type of picture—called a thermogram—displays the levels of heat in an object. Heat radiating from a person's hand is red. The air close to the hand radiates less heat and is shown in yellow. The surrounding cool air is colored blue.

CHAPTER ONE

What Is Heat?

HEAT IS EVERYWHERE

Everything around you is made up of very tiny **atoms**. Atoms are considered the building blocks of all matter, and join together to form larger particles called **molecules**. Both atoms and molecules are capable of holding internal energy, which makes atoms and molecules move. These particles will move faster as their energy increases.

Heat is a form of energy that causes atoms and molecules to move. Hot molecules have more internal energy and move faster. Cold molecules have low levels of internal energy and move very slowly. Molecules with large amounts of internal energy will release some of their energy. This energy increases and spreads as an object is warmed. There are three ways in which heat energy can travel: **conduction, convection,** and **radiation.**

CONDUCTION

During conduction, heat energy is directly passed along from one particle, such as an atom or molecule, to another. The particles must actually touch to spread the heat energy. Hot particles with high internal energy move faster and bump into cooler particles. The cooler particles begin to move faster as their heat energy increases. This movement causes them to bump into more particles, spreading the heat energy.

Some materials, such as metals, conduct heat well. For example, if you reach for a metal object, such as a spoon, it might feel cold when you first touch it. The metal is rapidly conducting heat away from your hand. The coldness you feel is your hand losing heat.

A blacksmith uses long metal tongs to hold a horseshoe that he is heating over an open fire. Heat from the shoe travels by conduction through the tongs but lessens rapidly with distance. The tongs are long enough for him to hold the shoe safely.

Eventually, the metal spoon will become warmer as the object conducts more heat.

Other materials, such as wood and plastic, do not conduct heat as well as metal and are considered poor conductors. If you held a wooden or plastic object, it would feel warm because it is not rapidly conducting heat away from your body. The warmth you are feeling is actually your own warmth. In order to heat poor conductors, you would need to apply larger amounts of heat energy over a longer period of time. Handles of metal cooking pans are often made of a special type of plastic. This allows a person to hold the pan while it is being heated. Without a handle made of a poor conductor, a person could burn his or her hand.

CONVECTION

Like conduction, convection also has to do with the movement of material that has been heated. The process of heating a pot of cold water is a good way to explain convection. When the pot of water is put on the stove, heat travels from the stove to the bottom of the pot. The water inside eventually becomes hotter. But it is the water at the bottom of the pot that heats up first. As these water molecules heat up, they become lighter and move to the top of the pot.

The cooler water molecules are heavier, so they sink to the bottom to fill the space left by the lighter, hotter molecules. These cooler molecules are heated, and eventually move to the top. The process repeats itself over and over. The moving liquid makes a circular pattern called a **convection current.** If the pot is made of glass, you will be able to see these currents. The convection current will continue to move until all of the liquid is heated to the same temperature.

Convection can occur in both liquids and in the air. Breezes are produced by convection heating in the Earth's atmosphere. Convection currents even play a part in the strong winds of hurricanes.

A gas burner warms the bottom of a glass pot containing water. Warm water rises from the bottom and is replaced by cold water from the top, causing convection currents. Air dissolved in the water breaks free as bubbles when the water boils.

RADIATION

In radiation, extra heat energy from an atom or molecule is passed on as invisible rays or waves from inside the particles. The molecules do not need to touch to spread the heat energy. Because of this, radiation also allows heat energy to travel across a **vacuum.** A vacuum is a space that has no matter in it—no atoms, molecules, or any other types of particles.

Heat rays from the Sun travel through space to warm our Earth.

INSULATION

To keep an object or an area at a specific temperature, a person must prevent heat from entering or leaving. This is called insulation. There are different ways a person can insulate things.

Convection can be slowed down by preventing the movement of warm and cold molecules. This can be done by placing something between hot

Radiation allows heat energy from the Sun to travel through millions of miles of space until it reaches Earth.

and cold areas. Scientists often use a material like a thick gel in between these spaces. A vacuum or a space where air cannot move can also be used to block convection. Many houses have special windows that help insulate the house. These windows have two layers of glass, with a gap of air between them. This air helps to slow down convection.

To reduce heat loss in a house, sheets of fiberglass (shown in pink) can be used as an insulator.

Insulating with a poor conductor is also helpful. Wooden or plastic handles on hot metal pots are some examples. The walls of houses are sometimes wrapped in a material called fiberglass. This is a material that prevents or slows down heat conduction between the outdoors and the indoors. Well-insulated houses do not need as much extra heat to remain warm in the winter. Similarly, insulation can help keep a home cool during warmer months.

Another form of insulation effectively blocks heat from traveling through conduction, convection, or radiation. In the late 1890s, Scottish scientist James Dewar created a covered **flask**—a type of container that holds liquids—to keep chemicals cold. The tight cover—made of cork, wood, or some other poor conductor—prevented heat from escaping or entering through the top. The flask had two walls, with a vacuum between them. Since the vacuum had no molecules, it was harder for heat to escape or enter the flask through the empty space. To prevent radiation from moving the heat, the flask was covered in a silvery or shiny coating. This coating reflected the heat rays away from the flask. Since Dewar's time, scientists have improved the way these flasks are made and the quality of the materials used, but the basic idea remains the same. Today we know these flasks as thermoses.

A colored X ray of a thermos reveals the different layers used to insulate the liquid inside (shown in red).

This thermoscope was built during the nineteenth century, following Galileo's original design.

CHAPTER TWO

Measuring Temperature

Temperature is a measurement of an object's heat. However, temperature is not the *amount* of heat contained in an object, but the *level* of that heat energy. At high temperatures, molecules and atoms move quickly and radiate excess internal energy, which travels as heat. At low temperatures, atoms and molecules move slowly. A gallon of cold water may have a higher amount of heat than a hot cup of water, because there are more molecules in the gallon and each molecule has some heat. But the cup of hot water has a higher temperature because the molecules—though there are fewer—are moving faster and radiating more heat energy.

Humans have always been able to tell the difference between hot and cold. But until the 1500s, people were unable to measure temperature. Eventually, scientific progress led to a better under-standing of heat and the technology to measure it.

THE THERMOSCOPE

One of the first recorded attempts to measure differences in tempera-ture was made by the Italian scientist Galileo Galilei in 1592. Galileo wanted to measure the difference in temperature between two rooms. To perform his experiments he used a glass flask with a long thin neck and a bulb-shaped bottom and a separate container of colored liquid. Galileo gently warmed the bottom of the flask, which caused the air inside to expand and travel up the thin neck. He then turned the flask upside down and put it in the container of colored liquid. As the air inside the flask cooled, it shrank and moved up toward the flask's bulb. This movement pulled the liquid up the neck of the flask.

Galileo brought his apparatus into a warm room and noted how the colored liquid moved up or down the neck of the flask. Then he moved into a colder room. The air inside the flask cooled, and the colored liquid rose higher. He compared the new level with the original one. The difference between the levels gave him a feel for the temperature difference between the rooms. Scientists refer to Galileo's apparatus as a thermo-scope. (*Thermo* refers to heat and *scope* refers to a device used to observe something.)

This engraving from the 1700s shows a scientist measuring temperature with an early thermometer. This thermometer was similar in design to Galileo's thermoscope.

This device is called a slow thermometer and has different weights floating in a tube of water. Cold liquids support floating weights better than warm liquids because the molecules in cold liquids are packed close together. The weights in this device settle at different levels depending on how heavy they are. The lowest weight indicates the room temperature. Galileo's studies and experiments with heat and temperature included the scientific principles that make this type of thermometer work.

MAKE YOUR OWN THERMOSCOPE

By following these instructions you can make your own version of a simple thermoscope.

Materials:
One small empty water bottle (about 11 ounces to 20 ounces in size)
Tap water
Rubbing alcohol
Food coloring (only one color is needed)
One clear plastic drinking straw
Modeling clay

Estimate how much liquid you would need to fill one quarter of the empty water bottle. Half of that amount will be made up of tap water and the other half will be rubbing alcohol. Combine the two liquids in your empty water bottle and put in a few drops of food coloring. Carefully swirl the mixture around until the color is spread out. Cover the bottle with its plastic cap while you are preparing the other parts of the experiment.

Break off and soften enough modeling clay to plug the opening of your water bottle.

mixture of rubbing alcohol and tap water

Uncover your bottle and insert the straw. The straw should go into the colored liquid, but be sure that the straw is not touching the bottom of the bottle. Use the clay to plug the bottle's opening and to keep the straw in place. Notice where the liquid is in the straw.

Hold the bottle in your hands to warm the air inside. What happens to the liquid in the straw? If you place the bottle on a windowsill or in the sunlight does the liquid level increase or decrease? What if you put the bottle in the refrigerator? Does the level in the straw go down? Use your thermoscope and think about what is happening to the air particles when they become warm and when they cool.

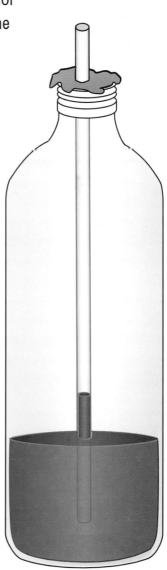

FAHRENHEIT AND CELSIUS

Galileo's thermoscope could show differences in temperature, but it did not actually measure temperature. Today temperature can be measured using degrees in two systems: Fahrenheit and Celsius.

FAHRENHEIT

The first thermometer was created in 1714 by a German scientist named Gabriel Daniel Fahrenheit. Fahrenheit used a glass tube that was almost completely filled with mercury. (He decided to use mercury instead of water because it responds quickly to temperature changes and expands or contracts evenly with those changes.) The tube of mercury was heated and then sealed. This left very little air inside the tube, creating a near-vacuum.

To record the levels of mercury in the tube at different temperatures, Fahrenheit put a scale—or markings—on the tube.

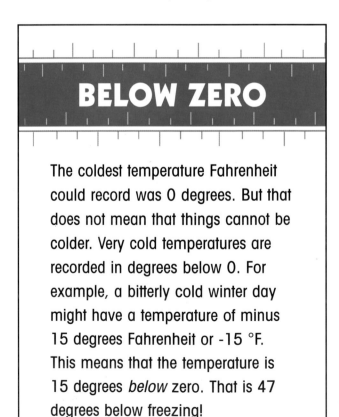

BELOW ZERO

The coldest temperature Fahrenheit could record was 0 degrees. But that does not mean that things cannot be colder. Very cold temperatures are recorded in degrees below 0. For example, a bitterly cold winter day might have a temperature of minus 15 degrees Fahrenheit or -15 °F. This means that the temperature is 15 degrees *below* zero. That is 47 degrees below freezing!

The markings represented different degrees. He chose three points as his main markers. Zero was for the lowest temperature he could get, which was the reading for ice mixed with salt. The hottest temperature he could record—for boiling water—was 212 degrees. In between the two points, he noted that water froze at 32 degrees. Temperatures measured using Fahrenheit's scale are usually recorded as degrees Fahrenheit. So using that scale, you would say that water boils at 212 degrees Fahrenheit (212 degrees F or 212 °F, for short.)

In the United States, Fahrenheit's system is used for everyday use. Body temperature, room temperature, and oven settings are measured with it. American meteorologists also use the Fahrenheit system when discussing weather.

CELSIUS

Most scientists in the United States and scientists and people in other countries use the Celsius scale. This system of measuring temperature was named after the Swedish astronomer Anders Celsius. In 1742 he divided the basic temperature scale into 100 degrees. On his scale, water freezes at 0 degrees Celsius (0 °C) and boils at 100 degrees (100 °C). This system was originally called the centigrade scale because of its one hundred divisions (*centi* refers to one hundred). The Celsius scale is part of a larger measuring system called the metric system. The metric system is used by scientists and other people throughout the world.

TEMPERATURE CONVERSIONS

To convert temperatures in Fahrenheit and Celsius you need to do a little bit of math.

If you have a Fahrenheit temperature that you want to convert into degrees Celsius, you must first subtract 32 and then divide that number by 1.8 or (9/5). If "F" represents the temperature in Fahrenheit, you can use this equation:

(F - 32) ÷ 1.8 = temperature in Celsius

So if you want to convert 122 °F into degrees Celsius you would do this:

(122 - 32) ÷ 1.8 = 50 °C

If you want to convert a Celsius temperature into degrees Fahrenheit you first multiply by 1.8 (or 9/5) and then add 32. If "C" represents the temperature in Celsius, you can use this equation:

(C x 1.8) + 32 = temperature in Fahrenheit

So if you want to convert 55 °C into degrees Fahrenheit you would do this:

(55 x 1.8) + 32 = 131 °F

FREEZING POINT, MELTING POINT, AND BOILING POINT

All matter can be found in different **states**: solid, liquid, or gas. The state in which an object remains depends on the level of heat energy it holds.

For example, if you leave an ice cube in a bowl on the kitchen table, it will take up heat from the room. Its molecules rearrange themselves and the ice turns into water. Boil that water in a pan, and its molecules move faster and faster. Eventually, the water turns into steam. The particular temperatures at which these states change from one to another are called the freezing point, melting point, and the boiling point.

The freezing point is the temperature at which a substance turns into a solid. Water turns into solid ice at 32 °F (0 °C). The heat levels in these water molecules are so low that the molecules can no longer move around. The molecules stay in basically the same position, creating a solid. But not every substance turns into a solid form at 32 °F. Pure liquid mercury, for example, will solidify, or become a solid, at around -37.7 °F (-38.7 °C). Gases turn into solids at even lower temperatures. The lowest possible temperature—at which all of a substance's atoms and molecules are practically at a standstill—is called **Absolute Zero**. Scientists have found that Absolute Zero occurs at -495 °F (-273 °C).

Many solids will melt into liquid as heat energy is added. The increased heat energy raises the temperature, and molecules can move around to form a liquid. Interestingly, a substance's melting point is almost exactly the same temperature as its freezing point. The melting point for ice and freezing point for water is 32 °F (0 °C). Some chemical elements, such as lead, have very high melting points. Pure lead will remain in solid form until it is heated to a scalding 621.7 °F (327.6 °C)! Some solids do not melt into liquids. When high levels of heat are applied, these **flammable** substances will burn. Wood is an example of a flammable material.

Add enough heat, and a substance will boil. When it boils, it changes state and becomes a gas. This is called the boiling point. Water's boiling point is 212 °F (100 °C). When water boils, it changes from a liquid to steam or water vapor. However, some liquids can change into gas without reaching their boiling points. This happens through evaporation,

EXPERIMENTING WITH FREEZING POINTS

Freezing points vary from substance to substance. You can change a liquid's freezing point by changing its chemical makeup. This experiment will show you how regular table salt (a mixture of the elements sodium and chlorine) affects water's freezing point.

Materials:
Two ice cube trays
1 cup of water
1 tablespoon of salt

Pour 1/2 cup of water into one of the ice trays.

Mix 1/2 cup of water with the salt. Pour this mixture into the other ice tray.

Place both trays into the freezer for five hours. When you check on the ice trays you will find that the plain water has frozen into ice cubes. But what has happened to the water and salt mixture? What conclusions can you draw about how salt affects water's freezing point?

and depends upon the properties of the liquid and the air around it.

Boiling points depend on the local **atmospheric pressure.** Atmospheric pressure is the measurement of the force of the air in the atmosphere, or how hard the air is pressing down on an object's surface. When you heat water, you raise the pressure of the air that is dissolved in the water. At the boiling point that pressure equals the atmospheric pressure.

Atmospheric pressure is greatest at **sea level** where the atmosphere is 6 miles thick. If you go up to higher elevations above

Some liquids boil at lower temperatures than others. In making maple syrup, some of the water in the sap collected from a sugar maple tree is boiled off. The liquid that has not boiled off is a syrup that is sweeter than the original sap.

sea level, the air pressure decreases. The lower the air pressure, the easier it is for a liquid to reach its boiling point. So liquids, such as water, will boil faster at higher altitudes. For example, Mexico City's elevation is around 7,546 feet (2,300 meters) above sea level. Because of the high altitude, water there will boil at 199 °F (92.8 °C) instead of 212 °F (100 °C)! Fahrenheit was at sea level when he measured the boiling point of water. If he had lived in Mexico City or anywhere with a different elevation, his temperature scale would have been different.

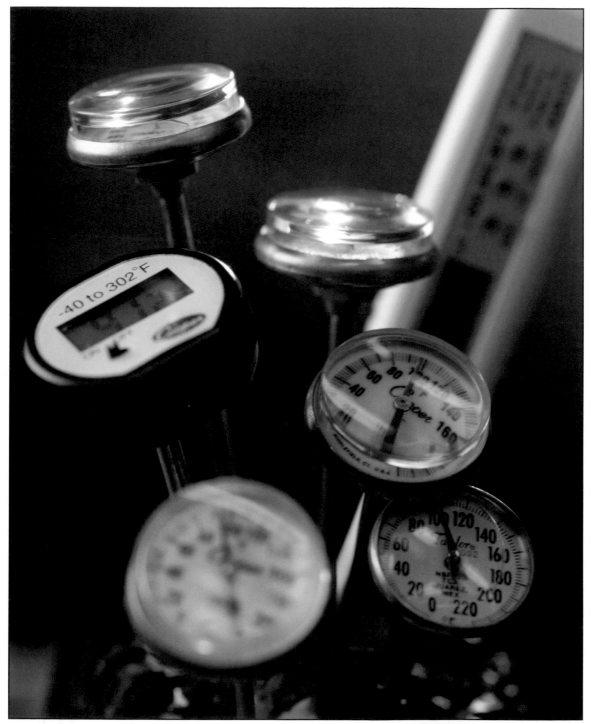

Thermometers may vary, depending upon their purpose and the temperatures they are supposed to measure.

CHAPTER THREE

Thermometers

Over the years, different types of thermometers have been invented for various purposes. Some were specially made to measure liquids, others to measure air, and still others for medical use. Very high or low temperatures require special equipment, also.

BULB THERMOMETERS

As their name implies, bulb thermometers have a bulb at the base, which leads to a long narrow tube that is sealed at the top. The bulb contains a colored liquid, often mercury or alcohol. As temperature increases, the liquid in the bulb expands and rises up the tube. Cold makes the liquid molecules contract, causing the liquid to move down the tube. Bulb thermometers are probably the most recognizable thermometers, and most people have some form of this thermometer in or around their homes. Many families mount bulb thermometers outside to gauge temperature.

CLINICAL THERMOMETERS

When you are sick, your parents or doctor might take your body temperature using a medical thermometer. These thermometers are designed to measure human body temperatures and they may take different forms.

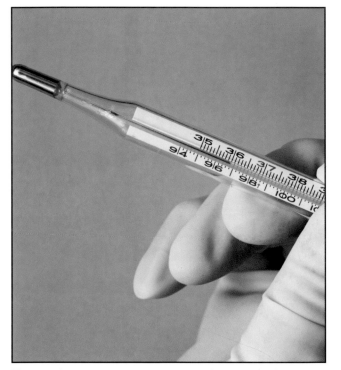

Mercury thermometers were very popular over the last century, but because of mercury's poisonous effects, most thermometers now use a different liquid.

The first thermometer used to measure body temperature was called a clinical thermometer and was a type of bulb thermometer. It was invented in the 1860s by Thomas Allbutt, a British doctor. He placed mercury in a sealed tube with a bulb at the bottom. Right above the bulb, the glass tube was heated and pinched tight so that only a small amount of mercury could pass through it. The mercury thermometer was placed against a person's body—sometimes under the tongue or beneath the armpit. The mercury would climb up the tube as it was heated. The pinched part of the thermometer helped keep the mercury at the measured level long enough for the doctor to read and record it. After the temperature was taken, the thermometer was shaken so that the mercury would flow down back to the bottom of the tube.

Scientists have since discovered that mercury can be poisonous. Today, most clinical thermometers use a different chemical instead of mercury. Many use alcohol or some other colored liquid.

But many parents and doctors no longer use this type of clinical thermometer—whether or not mercury is inside. Digital or electronic thermometers, which rely on **sensors** instead of a liquid traveling up a tube, are more often used. These thermometers are placed under the tongue or in the ear.

ELECTRICAL THERMOMETERS

Measuring things like body temperature or air temperature is simple using bulb thermometers. But how do we measure the temperature of something very hot, such as **molten** iron? An ordinary bulb thermometer would melt long before it even touched the iron.

To get around this, electrical thermometers were invented. These thermometers use electricity to gauge temperature. Electricity travels through matter in currents. Metals are very good at conducting electrical currents, but different types of metal

To measure high temperatures at the top of a volcano, scientists called vulcanologists need an electrical thermometer.

conduct electricity at different rates. How well a metal conducts electricity depends on its temperature. A piece of cold metal conducts electricity better than a hot metal piece. This is because heat and high temperatures fight against the electrical current, creating **resistance**. Metals at high temperatures offer more resistance against the current, and the current will be weaker. Electrical thermometers measure the strength or weakness of the electric current. If the current is meeting a lot of resistance due to high temperatures, the thermometer will register this.

RADIATION PYROMETER

Measuring the temperature of heat rays can be difficult because we can be hurt by those rays. A radiation pyrometer measures heat rays, so that scientists can be far from the rays' source. It was invented by a German engineer named Carl Wilhelm Siemens in 1861. A lens focuses heat rays onto a platinum wire that carries an

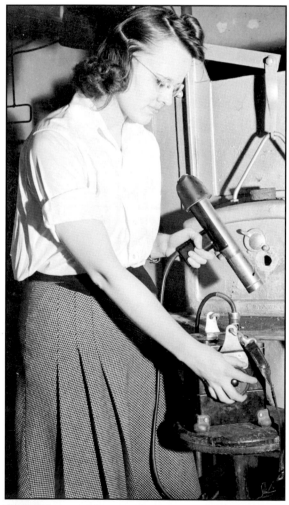

This photo was taken in 1941, as a scientist uses an optical pyrometer to study the properties of metals. Throughout the years, pyrometers have taken different forms, changing as technology improved.

electric current. When the heat rays warm the wire, the electrical resistance increases, and the current becomes weaker. The drop in current is measured and indicates the temperature. With a radiation pyrometer you can safely measure the temperature of very hot metals, such as molten iron. These pyrometers are also used to measure the temperature of burning gases from a rocket when it is launched.

Modified radiation pyrometers can also measure the temperature of the Sun. Heat and light go hand in hand: the intensity of the Sun's

A worker heats a furnace to melt precious metals for recycling. Not knowing the melting point of metals would make his job nearly impossible.

heat is related to its light. The hotter something is, the more intense the light it emits. We can measure the Sun's heat from its light. However, the atmosphere blocks some of the light, so scientists sent radiation pyrometers up in rockets far beyond the Earth's atmosphere. These pyrometers were modified to measure light intensity. The readings were sent back as radio signals.

To determine the Sun's temperature, scientists compared these readings with light intensity from other very hot things. The scientists had measured molten platinum metal's light intensity to get a temperature of 3221.6 °F (1772 °C). By doing some calculations based on that measurement, they were able to figure out that the Sun's surface is nearly 11,000 °F (6093 °C). That is sixty times hotter than boiling water!

THE THERMISTOR

This is another kind of electrical resistance thermometer. It reacts to heat through conduction. Instead of platinum wire, a thermistor uses a semiconducting material. (A semiconductor is not as efficient as a conductor, but it is much more efficient than an insulator or something that prevents conduction completely.) Resistance in a semiconductor works the opposite way from resistance in a metal. As the semiconductor gets hotter its resistance to electric currents decreases. Cold will increase a semiconductor's resistance.

The semiconducting material is made into a sensor. This sensor can be in any shape or size, from an inch-sized disk to a tiny bead. It can even be small enough to fit inside a tiny needle!

If the sensor gets hot, the electric current flows more easily through connecting wires. When the sensor is cold, the current has a harder time flowing. Either way, the flow of current is converted to a temperature reading. Thermistors are very sensitive to temperature differences—they can detect changes as small

This tiny thermistor made of semiconducting material is supported by wires. A small electric current is sent through the wires. The level of the current is affected by the temperature of the semiconductor, which allows scientists to measure temperature.

as one-thousandth of a degree. This makes them useful for measuring very small temperature changes.

THE THERMOCOUPLE

The thermocouple is another electrical device used for measuring temperature. The thermocouple was discovered in 1823 by the German physicist Thomas Johann Seebeck. He joined the ends of pieces of two different conducting metals. The metals are joined in two places, called junctions. In order to use a thermocouple, you must know what the temperature at one of the junctions is. The other junction is the temperature that you are trying to measure. A thermocouple works because of a special property that some metals have. If two different metals are joined together with their junctions at different temperatures, an electric current is generated. The current flows through the metals. The amount of current is measured and converted into a temperature.

Thermocouples can measure high or low temperatures. Different metals are used to measure different ranges of temperature, because each metal has its own electrical properties. For temperatures up to 2012 °F (1100 °C), iron and copper wires are used. A thermocouple made of platinum and rhodium measures temperatures up to 3218 °F

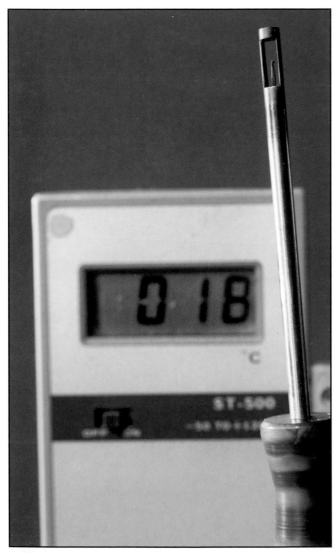

A thermocouple is used for sensing temperatures in a gas. The metal probe contains the thermocouple which is connected to a digital meter.

In 1997, the Mars *Pathfinder* carried thin wire thermocouples to Mars. One measured atmospheric temperature during descent. Three more were mounted on a mast that was raised after landing. These took temperatures of the thin Martian atmosphere at 10 inches, 20 inches, and 40 inches above the ground. The uppermost thermocouple registered 36 °F (2.2 °C) lower than the bottom thermocouple. If you stood on Mars, your nose would be much colder than your feet!

Pathfinder's electrical temperature readings were digitized and radioed to mission control. They revealed that we would not like to live on Mars. During what would be our early afternoon, the surface is a chilly 14 °F (-10 °C). Temperatures then fall to a low of -105 °F (-76 °C) just before the Martian sunrise.

The view from *Pathfinder* on the surface of Mars in 1997.

(1770 °C). Tungsten and rhenium thermocouples measure up to nearly 5432 °F (3000 °C). Other combinations allow us to measure very low temperatures.

THE BIMETALLIC THERMOMETER

This type of thermometer uses metal's expansion and contraction properties. All metals expand and contract with temperature, but by different amounts. A bimetallic thermometer uses two different types of metal strips.

In one form, strips of copper and iron are joined together to form a bimetallic strip. When the surrounding temperature changes, each metal expands or contracts differently. As a result, the bimetallic strip curves. The amount the strip curves depends on the temperature. The thermometer gauges these different curvatures and displays specific temperatures that represent each curve.

Bimetallic strips are

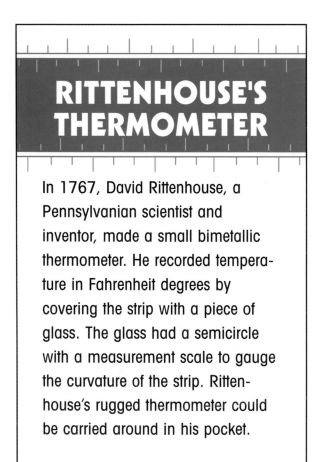

RITTENHOUSE'S THERMOMETER

In 1767, David Rittenhouse, a Pennsylvanian scientist and inventor, made a small bimetallic thermometer. He recorded temperature in Fahrenheit degrees by covering the strip with a piece of glass. The glass had a semicircle with a measurement scale to gauge the curvature of the strip. Rittenhouse's rugged thermometer could be carried around in his pocket.

common in dial thermometers used to measure air temperature. In a dial thermometer, the strip is coiled tightly into a spiral. As the temperature increases, the metal will expand and uncoil. A pointer is attached to the tip of the strip, and it moves as the strip moves, pointing to different temperatures on the dial.

A **thermostat,** which is used to regulate temperature and heat, contains a bimetallic strip. Many homes have room thermostats that

An outdoor dial thermometer contains a bimetallic strip. Depending upon where an outdoor thermometer is placed, the temperature it displays can sometimes be misleading. Direct sunlight or shade can alter temperature readings.

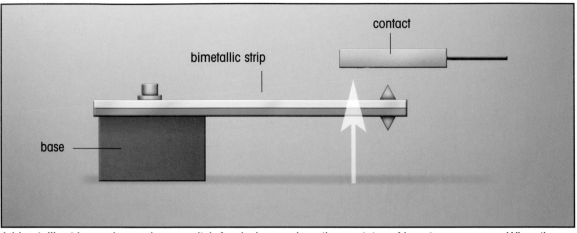

A bimetallic strip can be used as a switch for devices such as thermostats, refrigerators, or ovens. When the temperature changes, the strip will move toward or away from the contact. Once part of the strip touches the contact, the device will switch on.

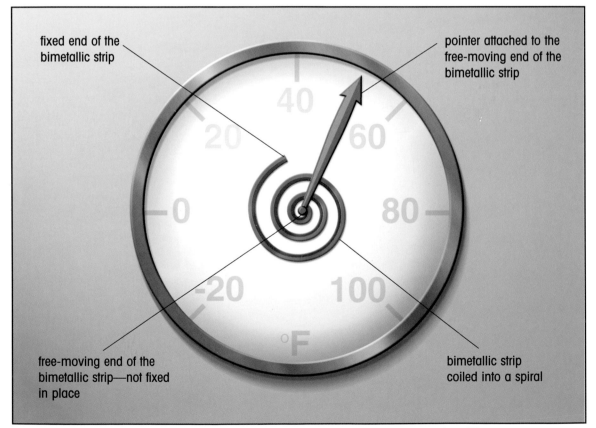

As the temperature changes, the coiled bimetallic strip will move the pointer, indicating different temperatures. The strip is shown in two colors to represent the two different types of metal used.

help to keep a house warm. The thermostat is set at a certain temperature. When the room temperature falls below the setting, the strip curves. The curved strip connects to a switch that turns on a furnace, which spreads heat throughout the house. When the room temperature goes back to the set temperature, the strip bends back and the furnace shuts off. This is just one of the many

Without thermostats, we would have a hard time adjusting and maintaining comfortable temperatures in our homes.

ways that thermometers help to make our lives more comfortable.

Instead of using a clinical bulb thermometer, body temperature can be measured with a digital thermometer that uses a thermistor powered by a tiny battery.

CHAPTER FOUR

How Temperature Affects You

BODY TEMPERATURE

Your body is made up of a complex network of cells, organs, and systems. In order for the cells to function properly, your body must maintain a certain temperature. The average human body temperature is around 98.6 °F (37 °C). Like a very sophisticated thermostat, your body has ways to make sure you maintain that temperature.

On very hot days or when you are moving around or exercising, your body temperature will increase. When your body gets too hot, your brain tells it to cool down, and you start to sweat to release heat. (You also learn that drinking a cold drink, using a fan or air conditioner, or taking a cold shower or quick swim will help cool you down, too.) If you do not cool down, your cells start to malfunction and some even die. This can cause organ damage and death. So it is very important that you try not to get too hot.

There are times, however, when your body will increase its temperature on purpose. Fevers are a body's natural reaction to illness or infections. For example, if your body is invaded by bacteria or viruses

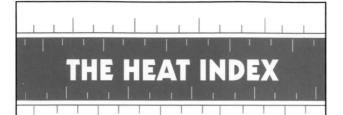

THE HEAT INDEX

Often, the heat you feel during warm months is not just from the air temperature. Humidity—the amount of moisture in the air—plays a part in how hot your body can get. When there is more moisture in the air on a hot day, the sweat from your body cannot evaporate easily. As a result, it takes a longer time for your body to cool. High temperatures and high humidity can be a dangerous combination if you are outdoors. This is one reason why scientists developed the heat index. The index is a system of calculations used to determine how hot it *feels* outdoors. The calculations take into account the actual air temperature and the air's relative humidity. This is why on certain days weather reports will say that the temperature is going to be in the eighties, but will feel like it is in the nineties. Knowing information like this can help you take the proper precautions when you are working or playing outside on a hot summer day.

that make you sick, you will most likely develop a fever. A fever is a significant rise in body temperature above the average 98.6 °F (37 °C). This increased heat is your body's attempt to kill the invading cells and to fight the infection. Often, a fever will go away on its own. However, very high fevers that last for a long time can be dangerous, and doctors will give a person medication to bring down the fever.

Exposure to extremely cold temperatures can cause serious health problems. So people have learned to use the theories behind insulation to stay warm—from insulating a house to wearing a thick winter coat. Also, when you are cold, your body finds ways to generate heat and increase your internal temperature. Shivering is a natural reaction to the cold. Your brain tells your muscles to contract and shake, creating heat and raising your body temperature.

USING TEMPERATURE

We raise and lower temperatures to make our bodies and homes comfortable. But we also manipulate temperature to provide us with products that we need for our everyday lives.

Nearly all metals are solid at room temperature and many of them are difficult to bend or shape when they are solid. Manufacturing plants that use metals or alloys (a mixture of different metals) to make their goods must know melting points and other temperature references. If the workers did not know what temperature is needed to melt steel or iron, how could they use the materials to make things like instruments, tools, and car parts?

CALORIES

You get your energy—and the ability to stay warm and maintain the right body temperature—through the food that you eat. When food is broken down in your body, it provides you with calories. A calorie is actually a measurement of energy, not temperature. But a calorie's definition is based on temperature: 1 calorie is the amount of energy needed to raise the temperature of 1 gram of water 1 degree Celsius.

Molten steel is poured into rectangular containers called patterns. As the steel cools, bars are formed. The temperature of the molten steel can be measured from a safe distance using a pyrometer.

Temperature also plays a role in sanitation—or keeping things clean. Many bacteria, viruses, or other dangerous microorganisms cannot survive at certain temperatures. Because we know this, we use hot water—along with cleaning agents like soap—to disinfect things. Machines have also been made to expose tools, such as medical instruments, to high temperatures in order to clean them.

Proper food safety also requires a knowledge of temperatures. High cooking temperatures for food like raw meat and eggs can help prevent illness and disease. Some foods must remain at low temperatures or they will spoil. Refrigerators and freezers have thermostats and

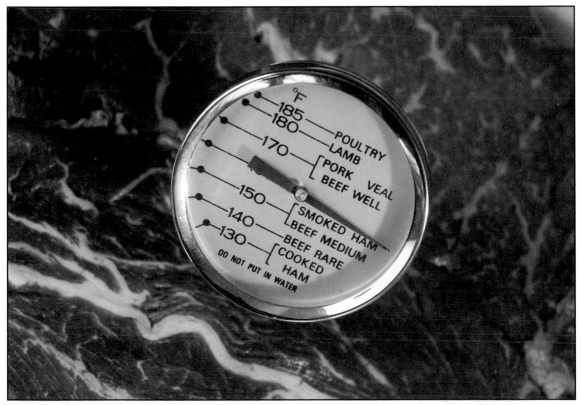

Many meat thermometers have helpful guides that show a person the temperature at which certain meats should be safely cooked.

From measuring body temperature to conducting experiments, thermometers are an essential part of our lives.

thermometers that help to maintain these temperatures. Health inspectors visit restaurants to check their cleanliness, and part of the inspection includes testing their freezer and refrigerator thermometers.

It is natural that many of us take temperature measurements for granted. We are so used to looking out the window at a thermometer or looking online or on television for the weather and temperature predictions. If we have fevers, it is often simple enough to grab a thermometer, take our temperature, and then take some medication to get better. But if it were not for the scientists throughout history who took the time to experiment with and learn about temperature, much of our modern progress would never have been possible.

GLOSSARY

atmospheric pressure—The measurement of how hard the air is pressing down on an object's surface.

atom—A small particle. Atoms are the building blocks of matter and join together to form molecules.

boiling point—The temperature at which a substance boils and turns into vapor.

conduction—The movement of heat through physical contact between molecules or atoms.

convection—The movement of heat through circulation of a fluid or gas.

convection currents—The circular pattern in which a substance moves when heat travels by convection.

flammable—Able to be set on fire and burn easily.

flask—A container or bottle used to hold liquids.

freezing point—The temperature at which a substance solidifies.

insulation—The process of preventing heat or cold from traveling through something.

melting point—The temperature at which a solid material becomes a liquid.

molecules—Small particles made up of two or more atoms.

molten—To be liquefied or melted by heat.

pyrometer—A thermometer that uses electrical resistance to measure high temperatures caused by radiation.

radiation—Energy—including heat energy—that is given off in the form of small particles or waves.

resistance—A force that works against the motion of another force. In electricity, a measurement of how easily an electric current passes.

sea level—The level of the ocean's surface. It is used to measure the depths of the oceans and land elevation or altitude.

sensor—A device that responds to a stimulus such as heat, light, pressure, or sound.

states (of matter)—The forms matter can take, including solid, liquid, or gas.

thermistor—A temperature-measuring device that works based on properties of electrical resistance.

thermocouple—A temperature-measuring device that generates an electric current from two different metals joined at their ends. Each metal is at a different temperature.

thermostat—A device that controls temperature.

vacuum—A space that is completely empty—there are no solids, liquids, or gases.

FIND OUT MORE

BOOKS

Farndon, John. *Solids, Liquids, and Gases*. New York: Benchmark Books, 2002.

Gardner, Robert. *Really Hot Science Projects with Temperature: How Hot Is It? How Cold Is It?* Berkeley Heights, NJ: Enslow Publishers, 2003.

Lauw, Darlene. *Heat*. New York: Crabtree Publishing Company, 2002.

Rodgers, Alan. *Temperature*. Chicago: Heinemann Library, 2003.

Sadler, Wendy. *Hot and Cold: Feel It!* Chicago: Heinemann-Raintree, 2006.

WEB SITES

Heat and Temperature
http://coolcosmos.ipac.caltech.edu//cosmic_classroom/light_lessons/thermal/index.html

Measuring Temperature
http://oncampus.richmond.edu/academics/education/projects/webunits/measurement/temp1.html

Temperature: Weather Wiz Kids
http://www.weatherwizkids.com/temperature.htm

INDEX

ABOUT THE AUTHOR
Navin Sullivan has an M.A. in science from the University of Cambridge. He lives with his wife in London, England, and has dedicated many years to science education. He has edited various science texts, and has written science books for younger readers. Navin Sullivan has also been the CEO of a British educational publisher and Chairman of its Boston subsidiary. His hobbies include playing the piano and chess.